BROTHERHOOD AND SMALL GROUPS

Brotherhood and Small Groups: A Culturally Responsive Curriculum for Boys is a transformative step-by-step guide for school counselors designed to empower young boys, particularly those from marginalized communities, with essential social, emotional, and leadership skills.

By offering an engaging, experiential curriculum, this program creates a safe space where boys can explore their identities, set meaningful goals, and overcome societal barriers. Unlike traditional resources, this book uniquely integrates culturally relevant practices and emphasizes community, accountability, and empathy. Group facilitators will be equipped with lesson plans, assessments to help monitor the effectiveness of their group, and the impact it has on school, community, and family.

Brotherhood equips educators and counselors with ready-to-use tools to nurture the next generation of leaders while fostering confidence, resilience, and a sense of belonging in every participant.

Brittany N. Glover, PhD, NCC, LCMHCA, NBCT, is a dedicated counselor, educator, researcher, and advocate for equity in education and mental health and an assistant professor at San Diego State University, CA.

BROTHERHOOD AND SMALL GROUPS

A Culturally Responsive Curriculum for Boys

Brittany N. Glover, PhD

Routledge
Taylor & Francis Group
NEW YORK AND LONDON

Designed cover image: Getty Images

First published 2026
by Routledge
605 Third Avenue, New York, NY 10158

and by Routledge
4 Park Square, Milton Park, Abingdon, Oxon, OX14 4RN

Routledge is an imprint of the Taylor & Francis Group, an informa business

Library of Congress Cataloging-in-Publication Data
Names: Glover, Brittany N. author
Title: Brotherhood and small groups : a culturally responsive curriculum
for boys / Brittany N. Glover.
Description: New York, NY : Routledge, 2026. | Includes bibliographical
references and index. |
Identifiers: LCCN 2025009009 (print) | LCCN 2025009010 (ebook) | ISBN
9781032531236 paperback | ISBN 9781003410409 ebook
Subjects: LCSH: Boys--Psychology | Boys--Education | Educational counseling
Classification: LCC LB1027.5 .G56 2026 (print) | LCC LB1027.5 (ebook) |
DDC 371.4--dc23/eng/20250714
LC record available at https://lccn.loc.gov/2025009009
LC ebook record available at https://lccn.loc.gov/2025009010

ISBN: 9781032531236 (pbk)
ISBN: 9781003410409 (ebk)

DOI: 10.4324/9781003410409

Typeset in Warnock Pro
by KnowledgeWorks Global Ltd.

Contents

Contents

Acknowledgments

I want to express my deepest gratitude to everyone who has supported me throughout the journey of creating this book. First and foremost, to my incredible Whitewater Academy family in Charlotte, NC, thank you for being a source of inspiration and encouragement. I am the school counselor educator I am today because of my school counseling journey at Whitewater. I am forever grateful for my Dolphin family.

To my parents, Rev. JD and Angela Glover, you have been my foundation and my guiding light. Your love, sacrifices, and belief in my vision have carried me through every challenge and triumph. I am endlessly grateful for your wisdom and encouragement.

To my mentors and esteemed colleagues, Dr. Sejal Foxx, Dr. Lyndon Abrams, Dr. Tabitha Haynes, Dr. Clare Merlin, Dr. Julius Ford, and Dr. Charmane Conner, thank you for sharing your knowledge, providing guidance, and believing in my potential. Your mentorship has been invaluable, and I am honored to have learned from such incredible leaders in education.

To my family, sorority sisters (Delta Sigma Theta Sorority Incorporated), friends, and NBCC and SDSU family and colleagues, thank you for your love, patience, and understanding as I dedicated time and energy to this work. Your encouragement has been a beacon of light, keeping me grounded and focused on this important mission.

This book is dedicated to the minority boys who *will* become the next generation of leaders. May this guide serve as a resource for the amazing school counselors and school personnel who will facilitate small groups, empowering these young men to achieve their fullest potential. Together, let us continue to create spaces where these boys can thrive, dream, and lead with confidence and purpose.

Thank you all for being a part of this journey.

The Significance of Culturally Responsive Boy Groups

Boys today are navigating a complex world filled with challenges and social pressures. We know boys to be adventurous, curious, spirited, energetic, playful, determined, and resilient. However, as they transition from childhood to adolescence, they are faced with the growing expectations of academic performance, social acceptance, and peer influence. Many boys encounter issues such as bullying, identity formation, and the pressure to conform to societal norms about masculinity (Reigeluth & Addis, 2020). Additionally, the growing uptick in the use of technology and social media introduces new complexities and pressures such as cyberbullying and unrealistic comparisons which affect decision making, self-esteem, and emotional well-being (Uhls et al., 2017). Moreover, for minority boys, these challenges can be compounded by cultural and societal barriers, making it even more critical for them to have access to support systems that encourage resilience, self-awareness, and confidence (Bryant et al., 2021).

Culturally responsive small groups for boys are essential because they provide targeted specific support for addressing the unique social, emotional, and academic challenges faced by minority boys. Research has shown that culturally tailored interventions can significantly improve academic outcomes and personal development for students of diverse backgrounds by fostering a space of belonging and empowerment (Hammond, 2020). Creating safe spaces where boys can explore their identities, share experiences, and receive guidance on how to navigate systemic barriers can lead to boys feeling more engaged at school, raise academic achievement and drop-out rates, and ultimately improve self-esteem and overall self-worth (Jones & Okun, 2019). Culturally responsive small groups incorporate cultural values and practices that not only resonate with diverse students' lived experiences; but the groups also help boys develop critical socio-emotional skills that potentially bridge gaps in emotional and behavioral development (Ladson-Billings, 2018).

Simply put, as educators and/or mentors, it is our responsibility to ensure that boys of diverse backgrounds are provided with interventions that address the inequities they face such as access to role models, a culturally relevant curriculum, and tailored emotional support (Gay, 2021). In an effort to close the opportunity gap, culturally responsive small groups represent a vital tool for supporting the development of boys from marginalized communities. Let us create culturally responsive groups so that our boys can thrive both in and out of the classroom.

About the Brotherhood Small Group Program

Purpose

The purpose of the Brotherhood small group is to provide a culturally responsive and inclusive program tailored to the unique needs of adolescent boys with an emphasis on minority boys. Through engaging and experiential activities, the program equips participants with practical tools for emotional regulation, goal setting, problem-solving, and leadership.

Objectives

By the end of the program, participants will:

- ❏ be equipped with tools to understand and manage emotions
- ❏ have cultivated leadership qualities
- ❏ have explored and celebrated their identities
- ❏ have set meaningful goals, identified barriers, and created actionable steps to achieve success (both within and away from the classroom)
- ❏ be equipped to communicate effectively, collaborate with others, and address common challenges with peer pressure, bullying, and societal expectations.

Overview

As mentioned above under purpose and objectives, the Brotherhood is a culturally responsive and inclusive curriculum designed specifically for upper elementary and middle school boys. The focus of the group is on supporting the unique needs of minority boys and draws on inspiration from culturally relevant practices. The program provides a safe space where boys can develop social, emotional, and leadership skills while exploring their identities. Brotherhood helps participants navigate the complex challenges they face, including peer pressure, bullying, and the expectations tied to masculinity, while encouraging pride in their heritage and fostering a strong sense of self-worth.

This small group program for boys provides engaging, interactive sessions utilizing an experiential approach. This approach aims to make learning more meaningful, practical, and impactful by having group members learn through activity and practice and by reflecting on their experiences from the activity. The group sessions/lessons offer structured activities and discussions that encourage personal growth and foster mutual respect among participants. Each session/lesson focuses on key areas such as emotional regulation, goal setting, problem solving, and leadership ensuring that boys leave with tools to succeed both inside and outside of the classroom. The program also focuses on community engagement and service while reinforcing values of empathy, accountability, and responsibility. The Brotherhood program ensures that each participant feels heard, valued, supported and prepared for the future.

The Brotherhood small group counseling program for boys is designed specifically for the busy school counselor or group facilitator who needs a 'ready to use' curriculum for their boys group. There are eight small group sessions/lessons provided. The tenth session/lesson serves as the culminating event or grand finale event. School counselors/group facilitators are encouraged to follow the lesson in sequence, as each lesson builds on another. However, school counselors/group facilitators are able to modify and select the lessons as they see to best align with their participants' needs.

Session Format

Each session/lesson is designed to last approximately 30–45 minutes, contingent upon group facilitators' time constraints. The sessions are aligned with the American School Counselor Association's (ASCA) lesson plan template. Each session is inclusive of the following:

- ❏ Student Learning Objectives (SLOs)
- ❏ Materials
- ❏ The Plan
- ❏ Do Now (*Warm-Up*)

❏ Activity
❏ Let's Talk About It (*Discussion*)
❏ Checks for Understanding

The session format is designed to be experiential in nature and provide consistency for both students and group facilitators.

Evaluations

Using pre-and post-test evaluations in small groups is an essential tool for group facilitators to assess the effectiveness of the small group. Pre-tests are used for all group facilitators to establish a baseline understanding of the students' knowledge, attitudes, and/or behaviors before the group begins, while post-tests help measure growth and change over time. This type of data-driven evaluation provides tangible evidence of a group's impact and enables counselors to adjust their approaches based on student needs (Sink, 2016). Moreover, research shows that evaluations can significantly improve program outcomes by identifying areas for refinement and ensuring that intended goals are being met (Dimmit et al., 2017).

In addition to formal evaluations, informal evaluations or checks for understanding such as exit tickets, journaling, and the 3-2-1 method (3 things learned, 2 things you would like more information/better understanding about, 1 question you have) held at the end of each group session provide immediate, quantitative and qualitative feedback. These tools give students an opportunity to reflect on their learning, express their feelings, and offer insights into the effectiveness of each session. This data can encourage continuous engagement and provide real-time data for the group facilitators to make more immediate adjustments to ensure objectives are being met and students' needs are best met (Dimmitt et al., 2017).

For the convenience of group facilitators, informal evaluations are included at the end of each lesson. Formal evaluations are located in Appendix A: Program Evaluations.

Preparing for a Small Group

Preparing for a small group can sometimes be a very challenging and daunting task. However, these steps aim to provide group facilitators with all they need to prepare for their group effectively. In addition, a checklist is also provided to assist in preparation.

Step 1: Logistics Preparation

Decide which grade level(s) are most needed for the Brotherhood Small Group.
Select a day, time, and place that the group will take place. Logistics recommendations are as follows:

- ❏ Small groups should meet at least once a week
- ❏ The duration of the group should be at least 35–45 minutes
- ❏ The group should consist of no more than 10 members
- ❏ The group should take place in a space that has the minimal distractions, yet provides space for movement and creativity.

Step 2: Call for Group Members

Reach out to the selected grade level(s) teachers and share some brief information about the upcoming potential group. Provide logistics information such as the day, time/duration, location of the small group. In addition, provide teachers with a recommendation form link (for example, Google Forms or Survey Monkey) so that they are able to recommend students they feel would benefit from the group. The form can also be shared with other staff and/or administrators within the school building. Once forms are received, select participants (recommended: no more than 10) to participate in the small group. Include a few alternate participants, in the event a participant expresses no interest in the group or does not return the parent/guardian permission form. The teacher recommendation email exemplar and the teacher recommendation form exemplar are in Appendix D.

Step 3: Participants and Parent/ Guardian Permission

Once all participants have been selected for the small group, meet briefly with each student to share information and expectations of the group, confirm their interest in the group, and to provide them with a parent/guardian permission form. Explain to students that the permission form needs to be signed and returned in order to participate in the group. The parent/guardian permission form exemplar can be found in Appendix D.

Step 4: Preparing Materials for the Group

While permission slips are waiting to be collected and returned, begin preparation for the lessons and ensure all materials have been secured. The text for each lesson includes a list of the necessary materials needed and also any handouts needed. Follow the **Quick Reference Session Preparation Guide**. It is highly recommended and best practice to prepare as many if not all materials prior to starting the small group in an effort to be effective and prepared for each session.

Step 5: Get Started!

Once group facilitators have received the parent/guardian permission forms, remind students, teachers, and any other necessary stakeholders about the logistics of the group (start day and time, location, etc.) and how students will be collected for the group (e.g., walk to group on their own or counselor/facilitator will collect them from their classroom).

About the Author

Brittany N. Glover, PhD, NCC, LCMHCA, is an assistant professor at San Diego State University, CA, and a dedicated social justice forward advocate for student success and empowerment. With six years of experience as a school counselor at Whitewater Academy in Charlotte, NC, Dr. Brittany brings a wealth of practical expertise to her work. She holds a Bachelor's degree in Psychology from Hampton University, a Master of Science in Counseling (School Counseling) from North Carolina A&T State University, and a PhD in Counselor Education and Supervision from the University of North Carolina at Charlotte.

Dr. Brittany's professional background spans elementary and high school counseling, providing her with a comprehensive understanding of students' developmental and academic needs. She is a licensed K-12 Special Education Teacher (NC), K-12 School Counselor (NC), and Licensed Clinical Mental Health Counselor Associate (NC).

An accomplished scholar and presenter, Dr. Glover has shared her expertise on both international and national stages, including the American School Counselor Association (ASCA), the National Board of Certified Counselors (NBCC), the American Educational Research Association (AERA), and the Association for Counselor Education and Supervision (ACES). She has publications in the areas of multicultural counseling, social justice school counseling, and preparing school counselors to serve students with special needs.

Beyond her professional pursuits, Dr. Brittany enjoys cooking, traveling, exploring diverse restaurants, and spending quality time with her loved ones. She is passionate about helping others grow and thrive, and her work continues to inspire and support the next generation of students and educators.

SESSION LESSON PLANS

Brotherhood

DOI: 10.4324/9781003410409-2

SESSION 1: BROTHERHOOD

Student Learning Outcomes
❏ Students will identify and establish key group norms for successful collaboration and respect within the group.
❏ Students will develop trust-building skills by participating in a guided obstacle course activity.
❏ Students will reflect on their role as both a listener and a communicator, identifying personal areas for improvement.

Materials Needed
❏ Folders or notebooks (*for storing worksheets, journal entries, handouts*)
❏ Brotherhood Oath document (*for students to sign*)
❏ Group member pre-test (*for assessment*)
❏ Poster paper or large paper (*to write down group norms*)
❏ Markers (*for writing norms on poster paper*)
❏ Blindfolds (*for trust-building obstacle course activity*)
❏ Desks/chairs/cones (*for setting up the obstacle course*)
❏ 3-2-1 Reflection Sheets or Written on Board/Poster (*for reflection and checks for understanding*)

Worksheets Included
❏ Brotherhood Small Group Purpose & Objectives Information Sheet
❏ Brotherhood Confidentiality Agreement
❏ Brotherhood Oath
❏ Brotherhood Group Norms Worksheet
❏ Session 1: Check for Understanding Worksheet
❏ Session 1 Parent/Guardian Letter

Session 1: Lesson Plan

First Day Preparation

1. Start the session/lesson by explaining the purpose and objectives of the group and ask the boys if they have any questions. Be sure to share how often the group will meet, the procedures for getting to the group each session/lesson, and when the group will end.
2. By demonstrating first, have each boy introduce themselves and provide an adjective or word that describes them. To make this a little challenging, have them use an adjective that starts with the same letter as their first letter of their first name (e.g., 'Basketball Brandon' or 'Charming Chris').
   a. *Note: Even if students know each other's names prior to the small group, this is a good way for students to learn about each other.*
3. Provide each student with a folder or notebook/journal so that they are able to keep worksheets, journal entries and other handouts in one place.
   a. *Note 1: The notebook can be used as an interactive notebook where students are able to glue/staple worksheets into the notebook.*
   b. *Note 2: The group facilitator/group members can decide who will be responsible for notebooks/folders after each session.*
4. Confidentiality and Brotherhood Oath Overview: Review the meaning of confidentiality with group members and have them sign the Confidentiality Agreement and the Brotherhood Oath.
5. Have each group member complete the group member pre-test. Explain that the pre-test is used to assess where they are now. Also explain that it will help us to be able to see growth at the end of the group and if group facilitators need to modify or make adjustments to upcoming sessions/lessons.

Do Now

1. Share and explain that in order for each group to function effectively and respectfully, groups should establish norms or rules.
2. Ask each boy to write down a rule or group norm that should be followed by each boy in the group.
3. Have each group member share their rule or group norm. As they are sharing, write the group's norms on poster paper/big paper. For rules/norms that are shared more than once, put a checkmark.

4. Once all group members have shared, have the group members vote on the top three to five norms. Once group members have voted and decided, have each group member sign the group norms on the poster paper/big paper to signify that they agree, they understand the group norms, and they will abide by them at all times.

Activity

Facilitator preparation: Create a maze or obstacle course for students. This can be as simple as rearranging desks/chairs around the room.

Instructions:
1. Have students pair with each other.
2. One student will need to be blindfolded and the other student will serve as their guide. (Idea: 'Rock, paper, scissors' can be used to determine who will go first.)
3. Instruct blindfolded students that they are going to be responsible for canceling the noise of others and focusing on the voice of their unblind-folded partner.
4. Instruct unfolded students that they are going to guide their partner across the classroom by instructing them where to walk, when to kneel and crawl, etc. They are responsible for ensuring that their partner makes it across the room without bumping into anything. They are not allowed to touch their partner; they can only use their words.
5. Students will switch roles when they get to the other side of the room to make it back to where they started.
6. The pair that finishes first wins.

Let's Talk About It

Questions for discussion:
1. What was it like to trust someone else to guide you?
2. What was it like to be responsible for your partner making it to the other side safely?
3. What was it like having to only listen to your partner, while hearing others provide directions to their partners?
4. Did this activity require a level of trust between you and your partner?
5. What can you take away from this activity as it relates to being a listener and being a communicator?

CHECK FOR UNDERSTANDING

3-2-1: Have students complete the 3-2-1 on a reflection sheet to go into their folders or in their notebook journals.

- ❏ **3** things you learned about being a listener/communicator today.
- ❏ **2** ways you can show your group mates they can trust you.
- ❏ **1** thing you need to continue working on as it relates to how you listen and or communicate.

Brotherhood Small Group: Purpose & Objectives Information Sheet

Brotherhood Small Group: Purpose

The purpose of the Brotherhood small group is to provide a culturally responsive and inclusive program tailored to the unique needs of adolescent boys with an emphasis on minority boys. Through engaging and experiential activities, the program equips participants with practical tools for emotional regulation, goal setting, problem solving, and leadership.

Brotherhood Small Group: Objectives

By the end of the program, participants will:
- ❏ be equipped with tools to understand and manage emotions
- ❏ have cultivated leadership qualities
- ❏ have explored and celebrated their identities
- ❏ have set meaningful goals, identified barriers, and created actionable steps to achieve success (both within and away from the classroom
- ❏ be equipped to communicate effectively, collaborate with others, and address common challenges with peer pressure, bullying, and societal expectations.

Brotherhood Confidentiality Agreement

I understand that what is said in this group should remain confidential within the Brotherhood group. I will not share what has been said by other participants with others outside the Brotherhood group. I understand that if I break this agreement, I may be asked to leave the group, indefinitely.

Student signature/Date

✂ -- ✂ CUT HERE

Brotherhood Confidentiality Agreement

I understand that what is said in this group should remain confidential within the Brotherhood group. I will not share what has been said by other participants with others outside the Brotherhood group. I understand that if I break this agreement, I may be asked to leave the group, indefinitely.

Student signature/Date

Brotherhood Oath

I am _____ [**Student Name**]

I am strong, courageous, and intelligent.
I am my brother's keeper!
I lead with integrity and empathy.
I celebrate who I am and where I am from.
I always strive for excellence.

I, _____ [**Student name**] promise to live by these affirmations.

Student signature _____

Date _____

✂ -- ✂   CUT HERE

Brotherhood Oath

I am _____ [**Student Name**]

I am strong, courageous, and intelligent.
I am my brother's keeper!
I lead with integrity and empathy.
I celebrate who I am and where I am from.
I always strive for excellence.

I, _____ [**Student name**] promise to live by these affirmations.

Student signature _____

Date _____

Brotherhood Group Norms Worksheet

Write down the group norms that your group decided on. Be sure to keep this so that you are able to reference them when needed.

Group Norm #1	
Group Norm #2	
Group Norm #3	
Group Norm #4	
Group Norm #5	

Session 1: Check for Understanding Worksheet

3-2-1

Answer the following questions:

- ❏ **3** things you learned about being a listener/communicator today
- ❏ **2** ways you can show your group mates they can trust you
- ❏ **1** thing you need to continue working on as it relates to how you listen and or communicate

Session 1: Brotherhood Small Group: Building Trust & Group Norms

Parent/Guardian Letter

Dear Parent/Guardian,

Today, _____ [student name] participated in the first *Brotherhood* small group session, where we focused on building trust, respect, and collaboration. The boys worked together to create group norms, establish expectations, and engage in a trust-building obstacle course. This activity helped them reflect on the importance of communication, trust, and teamwork.

Here's how you can reinforce this at home:

- ❏ Ask your child about the group norms they created and how they plan to follow them.
- ❏ Encourage open discussions about what trust means in friendships and family relationships.
- ❏ Practice active listening by taking turns sharing and summarizing each other's thoughts.

Thank you for supporting your child's participation in *Brotherhood Small Group*.

Ready, Set, Mindset

Setting Goals & Academic Excellence

DOI: 10.4324/9781003410409-3

SESSION 2: READY, SET, MINDSET
Setting Goals & Academic Excellence

Student Learning Outcomes
❏ Students will develop SMART goals for both academic and personal growth.
❏ Students will identify strengths and resources that can help them achieve their goals.
❏ Students will predict and analyze any potential obstacles that might impact them as they are working towards their goals
❏ Students will develop problem-solving skills to best navigate challenges and obstacles that may prevent them from achieving their goals.

Materials Needed

❏ 5 large poster boards or easels (*for each checkpoint station*):
  - Label each board with the specific checkpoint and instructions:
    - ○ Checkpoint 1: SMART goals (Create one academic and one personal goal)
    - ○ Checkpoint 2: Strengths and resources
    - ○ Checkpoint 3: Obstacles and challenges
    - ○ Checkpoint 4: Strategies to overcome challenges
    - ○ Checkpoint 5: Rewrite and commit to your goal
❏ Pens/pencils (*enough for all students*)
❏ Student journals/notebooks or loose-leaf paper
❏ SMART goals practice worksheets
❏ Music playlist (*optional, playing softly in the background to set the mood*)

Checkpoint station materials:

❏ Checkpoint 1 (SMART goals):
  - Printed SMART goal templates (*enough for each student*)
❏ Checkpoint 2 (Strengths and resources):
  - ○ Strength and resource identification sheets (*a simple worksheet with prompts to list their strengths and resources*)
❏ Checkpoint 3 (Obstacles and challenges):
  - ○ Obstacle identification sheets (*for students to write down challenges they foresee*)
❏ Checkpoint 4 (Strategies to overcome challenges):
  - ○ Strategy development sheets (*for brainstorming ways to overcome obstacles*)
❏ Checkpoint 5 (Mountain peak/overlook):
  - ○ Final goal sheet templates (*clean and aesthetically pleasing templates for students to rewrite their goals and sign them*)
  - ○ Frames or construction paper (*optional, for students to 'frame' their goals and display them*)

Worksheets Included
❏ Session 2: Do Now Worksheet
❏ Checkpoint Stations 1–5 label materials
❏ SMART Goals Practice Worksheet (*Part 1*)
❏ SMART Goals Practice Worksheet (*Part 2:* Checkpoints Worksheet)
❏ SMART Goals Practice Worksheet (*Goal Hike Mountain Activity*)
❏ Goal Hike Mountain Frame
❏ Session 2: Check for Understanding Worksheet
❏ Session 2: Parent/Guardian Letter

Session 2: Lesson Plan

Preparation: Prior to students coming to the group, prepare the room for the 'Goal Hike'. There should be five stations (known as 'checkpoints') for students to travel to. The 'checkpoint' stations should be set up as follows:

- ❑ Checkpoint Station 1: Students will create **one** academic goal and **one** personal goal using the SMART format.
- ❑ Checkpoint Station 2: Students will identify **one to three** (or more) strengths and resources that can help them reach their goal.
- ❑ Checkpoint Station 3: Students will identify at least **two** obstacles or challenges they may face attempting to achieve their goals.
- ❑ Checkpoint Station 4: Students will develop at least **one** strategy they can use to help them overcome their potential obstacle or challenge
- ❑ Checkpoint Station 5 (Mountain peak/overlook): Students will rewrite and 'frame their goal sheet' and then sign it, signifying their commitment to working on and achieving their goals.

Do Now (Warm-Up)

Have students answer the following questions in their notebooks or on a piece of paper for their folders:

- ❑ What is a goal?
- ❑ Are goals important to have? Why? Or why not?
- ❑ What is one goal you have this year?

Have each student turn and talk to their neighbor about what they have written. Then, allow students to share their answers aloud, with a small discussion. After the mini-discussion, explain to students how to set SMART goals using the SMART goals practice worksheet.

Activity

[Script] Now that we have learned how to create a SMART goal, each one of you is going to practice writing your own. Each one of you is going to climb 'Goal hike mountain'. Each station will serve as a checkpoint station on the mountain, and you will have a specific task that will help you develop your SMART goal and create a solid plan to achieve your goals. You are encouraged to talk with each other about your goals at each station; however, each group member

is responsible for having their own goals. I will share the tasks for each checkpoint station, and they are posted at each checkpoint as well.

- ❏ Checkpoint Station 1: Create **one** academic goal and **one** personal goal using the SMART format.
- ❏ Checkpoint Station 2: Identify **one** strength and **one** resource that can help you reach your goal.
- ❏ Checkpoint Station 3: Identify **one** obstacle or challenge you may face attempting to achieve your goals.
- ❏ Checkpoint Station 4: Develop at least **one** strategy you can use to help overcome your potential obstacle or challenge.
- ❏ Checkpoint Station 5 (Mountain peak/overlook): Rewrite and 'frame your goal sheet' and then sign it. This signifies your commitment to working on and achieving your goals.

Let's Talk About It (Discussion)

Have students share their goals and the strategies they came up with to support their journey to their goals. Discuss with students the ways they can be present, support each other's goals and hold each other accountable.

CHECK FOR UNDERSTANDING

Journal: Have students write about their experience 'climbing up goal mountain peak' in their journal. Use the following questions as prompts:

- ❏ What was it like to go through each checkpoint and complete the tasks related to your goals?
- ❏ Why are your goals important to you?
- ❏ How can this group support you or hold you accountable as you work towards achieving your goals?

Session 2: Do Now Worksheet

Answer the following questions using complete sentences.

1. What is a goal?
2. Are goals important to have? Why? Or why not?
3. What is **one** goal you have this year?

✂ -- ✂ CUT HERE

Session 2: Do Now Worksheet

Answer the following questions using complete sentences.

1. What is a goal?
2. Are goals important to have? Why? Or why not?
3. What is **one** goal you have this year?

CHECKPOINT STATION 1:

Students will create one academic goal and one personal goal using the SMART format.

CHECKPOINT STATION 2:

Students will identify one to three (or more) strengths and resources that can help them reach their goal.

CHECKPOINT STATION 3:

Students will identify at least two obstacles or challenges they may face attempting to achieve their goals.

CHECKPOINT STATION 4:

Students will develop at least one strategy they can use to help them overcome their potential obstacle or challenge

CHECKPOINT STATION 5 (MOUNTAIN PEAK/OVERLOOK):

Students will rewrite and 'frame their goal sheet' and then sign it, signifying their commitment to working on and achieving their goals.

SMART Goals Practice Worksheet (*Part 1*)

A SMART goal is a structured approach to setting goals that ensures clarity, focus, and an actionable plan. SMART is a method that helps us set clear, specific, and achievable goals. It's actually an acronym, which means each letter stands for something. Let's break it down.

Specific	Be very clear and direct about what you want to do.	*Example:* I want to improve my science grade. *Instead of* 'I want to do better at school.'
Measurable	Be sure that you can show/prove you met your goal.	*Example:* I will improve my science grade from a C to an A.
Achievable	The goal is realistic and can be within the time you have decided.	*Example:* I will study for 1 hour a day. *Instead of* 'I will study for 5 hours a day.'
Relevant	The goal matters to you and is aligned with your path, morals, and/or values.	*Example:* I want to improve my science grade because I want to get into a good college.
Time-Bound	Be sure to set a deadline or timeframe to ensure there is urgency and focus for your goal.	*Example:* I will achieve this goal by the end of the grading period.

SMART Goal Examples:

Example 1 (Academic Goal)
By the end of December, I will improve my math grade from a C to an A.

Example 2 (Personal Goal)
By the beginning of next year, I will make purple belt in Karate.

SMART Goals Practice Worksheet
(Checkpoints Worksheet)

Goal Hike Mountain Activity

Complete the table during your 'Checkpoints' activity. Be sure to use the SMART acronym for both of your goals.

Academic Goal (Checkpoint 1):		
Strengths (Checkpoint 2)	**Obstacles (Checkpoint 3)**	**Resources (Checkpoint 3)**
Strategy/Plan (Checkpoint 4)		

Personal Goal (Checkpoint 1):		
Strengths (Checkpoint 2)	**Obstacles (Checkpoint 3)**	**Resources (Checkpoint 3)**
Strategy/Plan (Checkpoint 4)		

Goal Hike Mountain Frame

My Personal Goal is

_____

_____

_____

_____

My Academic Goal is

_____

_____

Session 2: Check for Understanding Worksheet

Journal Entry

Answer the following questions:

- ❏ What was it like to go through each checkpoint and complete the tasks related to your goals?
- ❏ Why are your goals important to you?
- ❏ How can this group support you or hold you accountable as you work towards achieving your goals?

Session 2: Ready, Set, Mindset: Setting Goals and Academic Excellence

Dear Parent/Guardian,

Today in our *Brotherhood* group, your child learned about goal setting and the power of having a growth mindset. They practiced creating SMART goals (Specific, Measurable, Achievable, Relevant, and Time-bound) and identified personal strengths and resources to help them achieve their goals.

How you can reinforce this at home:

❏ Ask your child about the goals they set in the group and discuss ways you can support them.
❏ Help your child break their goals into smaller, manageable steps and celebrate progress.
❏ Model goal setting by sharing a personal or family goal and working together to achieve it.

We appreciate your partnership in fostering a growth mindset.

✂ – ✂   CUT HERE

Session 2: Ready, Set, Mindset: Goal Setting & Academic Excellence

Dear Parent/Guardian,

Today in our *Brotherhood* group, your child learned about goal setting and the power of having a growth mindset. They practiced creating SMART goals (Specific, Measurable, Achievable, Relevant, and Time-bound) and identified personal strengths and resources to help them achieve their goals.

How you can reinforce this at home:

❏ Ask your child about the goals they set in the group and discuss ways you can support them.
❏ Help your child break their goals into smaller, manageable steps and celebrate progress.
❏ Model goal setting by sharing a personal or family goal and working together to achieve it.

We appreciate your partnership in fostering a growth mindset.

I Am Me!

Self-Identity & Confidence

DOI: 10.4324/9781003410409-4

SESSION 3: I AM ME!
SELF-IDENTITY & CONFIDENCE

Student Learning Outcomes
❏ Students will understand the importance of authenticity and self-acceptance.
❏ Students will identify and express personal strengths, values, and challenges.
❏ Students will demonstrate creativity in expressing their identity.
❏ Students will engage in meaningful group discussions and provide positive feedback to peers.
Materials Needed
❏ Classroom desks/tables (*for students to rest their heads and cover their eyes*)
❏ Facilitator's statement sheet (*list of statements for the heads-up activity*)
❏ 'Shield of _____' Worksheets (*enough for each student, pre-printed*)
❏ Pens, pencils, crayons/colored pencils, markers
❏ Discussion prompts (*prepared in advance, can be written on the board or printed as a handout*)
❏ Reflection sheets (*3-2-1 format, enough for each student, or students can use their notebooks*)
Worksheets Included
❏ Shield Worksheet
❏ Session 3: Check for Understanding Worksheet
❏ Session 3: Parent/Guardian Letter

Session 3: Lesson Plan

Do Now (Warm-Up)

Preparation: Students will play a remixed version of Heads Up Seven Up (for confidentiality purposes).

Instruct: Ask students to put their heads down on their desk and cover their heads with their arms. Tell students to each leave one thumb accessible to give a 'thumbs up' if the statement said by the facilitator applies to them.

Facilitator: 'I am going to make a statement. If you agree with the statement, put your thumb up. If you do not, you will keep your thumb down. I will also let you know to lower your thumb after each statement. All heads should remain down until I have instructed you to lift your head. Are there any questions?'

Statements:
- ❏ 'I feel proud of who I am.'
- ❏ 'I feel comfortable being myself around my friends.'
- ❏ 'I feel comfortable being myself at school.'
- ❏ 'I feel proud of my cultural background and/or where I come from.'
- ❏ 'I sometimes feel pressured to change who I am to fit in.'
- ❏ 'I think it's important to stay true to yourself.'
- ❏ 'I find it difficult to be my true self at this school.'

Instruct: Inform students they can lift their heads. Have a brief whole group discussion regarding the statements and allow students to share the importance of being able to be their true selves.

Activity

Each student will receive a shield. This shield will represent who they are, their values, and their strengths. Students will first complete the pre-work for the shield worksheet. Have students identify the following on the worksheet and add their name in the blank at the top where it says 'Shield of_____'.

- ❏ **Strengths:** What are you good at?
- ❏ **Values:** What do you care most about?
- ❏ **Dreams:** What is your goal for the future? (Feel free to use a goal from the previous lesson.)

After students have completed the first part of the worksheet, they can utilize markers, pens, colored pencils, etc. to complete their shields showcasing their artistic creativity.

Let's Talk About It (Discussion)

After students have completed their shields, allow them to present their shields to the group. Encourage them to share their shields with pride about who they are. Encourage group members to compliment or provide positive feedback for their fellow group members after they have presented.

CHECK FOR UNDERSTANDING

3-2-1: Have students complete the 3-2-1 on a reflection sheet to go into their folders or in their notebooks/journals.

❑ Write **3** things that you learned yourself.
❑ Write **2** things that you learned about your group mates?
❑ Write **1** thing that you are going to take away and put into practice after this activity?

Session 3: Shield Worksheet

Shield of _____

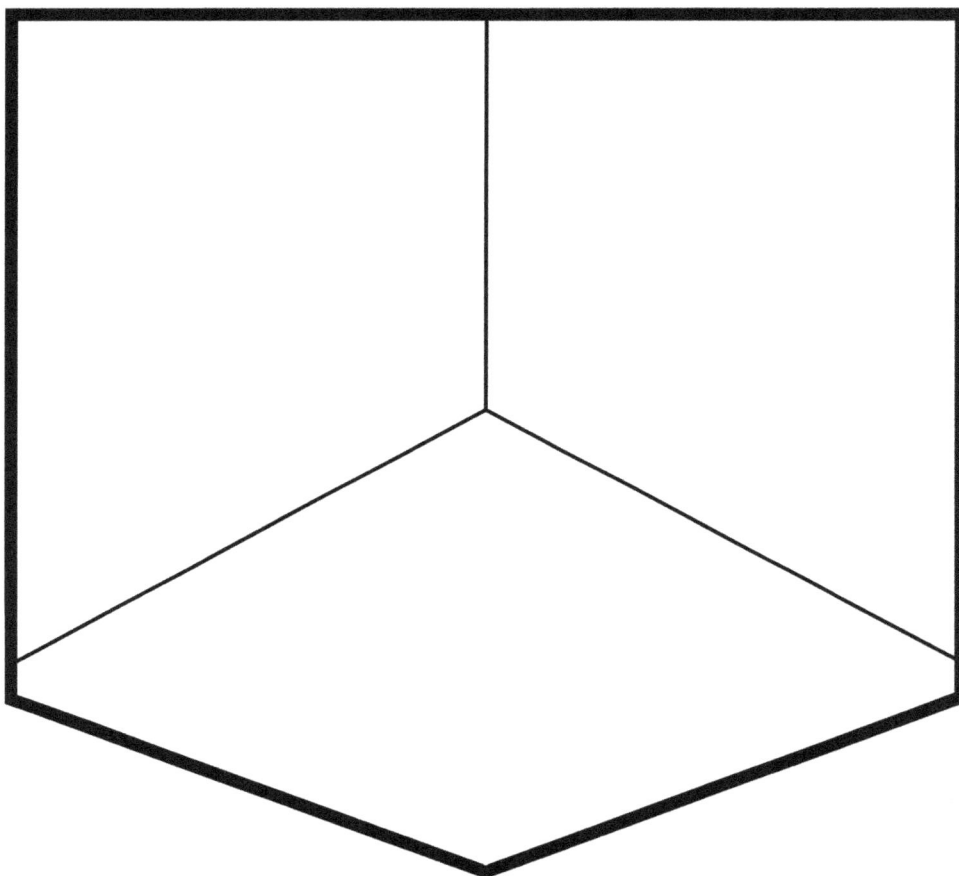

Session 3: Check for Understanding Worksheet

3-2-1

Answer the following questions:

- ❏ Write **3** things that you learned yourself.
- ❏ Write **2** things that you learned about your group mates?
- ❏ Write **1** thing that you are going to take away and put into practice after this activity?

Session 3: I Am Me! Self-Identity & Confidence

Dear Parent/Guardian,

In today's *Brotherhood* small group, we focused on self-identity and self-acceptance. The boys participated in a *Shield Activity*, where they reflected on their strengths, values, challenges, and dreams. This helped them celebrate their individuality and recognize what makes them unique.

How You Can Reinforce This at Home:

❏ Encourage your child to share their shield with you and explain what each section represents.
❏ Remind them of their strengths and how they positively impact others.
❏ Foster self-confidence by acknowledging their efforts and achievements, no matter how small.

Thank you for supporting your child's journey of self-discovery!

✂ ------------------------------------- ✂   CUT HERE

Session 3: I Am Me! Self-Identity and Confidence

Dear Parent/Guardian,

In today's *Brotherhood* small group, we focused on self-identity and self-acceptance. The boys participated in a *Shield Activity*, where they reflected on their strengths, values, challenges, and dreams. This helped them celebrate their individuality and recognize what makes them unique.

How you can reinforce this at home:

❏ Encourage your child to share their shield with you and explain what each section represents.
❏ Remind your child of their strengths and how they positively impact others.
❏ Foster self-confidence by acknowledging their efforts and achievements, no matter how small.

Thank you for supporting your child's journey of self-discovery.

Mindful of Me

Self-Control/Peer Pressure

DOI: 10.4324/9781003410409-5

SESSION 4: MINDFUL OF ME

Self-Control/Peer Pressure

Student Learning Outcomes
❏ Students will define peer pressure and identify examples of both positive and negative peer influences.
❏ Students will practice resisting peer pressure through role-play scenarios and understanding the consequences of their choices.
❏ Students will explore self-control techniques for managing emotions and impulses when experiencing peer pressure.
❏ Students will reflect on past experiences with peer pressure and develop strategies for making better decisions in the future.
Materials Needed
❏ Sticky notes (*one per student*)
❏ Markers or pens
❏ Poster boards or large paper labeled 'Positive Pressure/Influence' and 'Negative Pressure/Influence'
❏ Tug of War rope (*with a marked center point or ribbon to indicate the boundary*)
❏ Floor markers (*to mark the boundary line on the floor*)
❏ Index cards with peer pressure scenarios for each round:
■ Round 1 Scenario: Teasing for breaking rules
■ Round 2 Scenario: Cheating on a test
■ Round 3 Scenario: Fighting due to disrespect
❏ Journals or notebooks or loose paper if students are using personal folders
❏ Pens or pencils for writing
❏ Check for Understanding Worksheet
Worksheets Included
❏ Tug-Of-War Scenarios
❏ Session 4: Check for Understanding Worksheet
❏ Session 4: Parent/Guardian Letter

Session 4: Lesson Plan

Do Now (Warm-Up)

Ask students to write down the meaning of peer pressure. Then give each of them a sticky note to write down one way that a peer or someone on social media has influenced them in the past week. Once students have written a response on their sticky note, have them place their sticky note on the respective poster board in the room: Positive Pressure/Influence or Negative Pressure/Influence (explain that it is up to them to decide if they feel they were positively or negatively influenced).

Have students turn and talk to their neighbor about their definition of peer pressure. Have students share out with the whole group and discuss the peer pressure their group members have shared on the sticky notes. After discussion and confirming a clear definition of peer pressure the students will be divided into two groups for the activity.

Activity

Divide students into two teams (Team 1: Peer Pressure; Team 2: Resisting Peer Pressure).

Instruct students that they are going to play Tug-of-War: Pressure Edition. Explain to them that they will be presented with different peer pressure scenarios. For each scenario, students will have a tug of war. Explain to students: 'The Peer Pressure team represents the pressure trying to pull the individual towards bad decisions. The Resisting Pressure team represents the strength and confidence needed to resist peer pressure.' The team that pulls the rope over the marked boundary wins the round. The rounds are as follows:

Round 1:
- ❏ *Read scenario*: Your friends are teasing you because you don't want to break the rules. You begin to think about whether you should do it, so they don't think you are weak.
- ❏ Instruct students to begin pulling on the count of 3.
- ❏ Once the marker on the rope has passed the boundary, announce the winner.

Round 2:
- ❏ Have a student from the peer pressure team join the resisting pressure team.
- ❏ *Read scenario*: You didn't study for a test, but a classmate says they'll show you their paper with the answers.

❏ Instruct students to begin pulling on the count of 3.
❏ Once the marker on the rope has passed the boundary, announce the winner.

Round 3:

❏ Have a student from the resisting pressure team, join the peer pressure team.
❏ *Read scenario*: Someone says something about you that you feel is disrespectful. You do not like to be disrespected and your friends are pressuring you to fight the individual that disrespected you at the end of school.
❏ Instruct students to begin pulling on the count of 3.
❏ Once the marker on the rope has passed the boundary, announce the winner.

Let's Talk About It (Discussion/Reflection)

Have the students come back together to reflect and have a discussion. Facilitate the discussion by asking students the following discussion questions:

❏ How did it feel to be on each side of the rope?
❏ How does this activity relate to real-life situations with peer pressure?
❏ How can you demonstrate self-control when faced with peer pressure?/ What are some strategies for resisting peer pressure?
❏ Why is it important to practice self-control and overcome peer pressure?

CHECK FOR UNDERSTANDING

Journal: Have students write about a time when they were faced with peer pressure and gave in to it. Have them write about how they would use the skills they learned today to help them make a better decision if a similar situation presented itself.

Tug-of-War Scenarios

Note: *Facilitators can use this sheet or cut it into pieces to create index-like cards.*

Round 1 Scenario

Your friends are teasing you because you don't want to break the rules. You begin to think about whether you should do it, so they don't think you are weak.

Round 2 Scenario

You didn't study for a test, but a classmate says they'll show you their paper with the answers.

Round 3 Scenario

Someone says something about you that you feel is disrespectful. You do not like to be disrespected and your friends are pressuring you to fight the individual that disrespected you at the end of school.

Session 4: Check for Understanding Worksheet

Journal Prompt

1. Write about a time when you were faced with peer pressure and gave in to the peer pressure.
2. Write about how you would use the skills you learned today to help you make a better situation if a similar situation happened again.

Session 4: Mindful of Me: Self-Control/Peer Pressure

Dear Parent/Guardian,

Today's *Brotherhood* small group session focused on self-control and handling peer pressure. The boys participated in activities that helped them recognize the power of their choices and how to resist negative influences. They also discussed ways to remain true to themselves in challenging situations.

How you can reinforce this at home:

- ❏ Talk to your child about a time when they faced peer pressure and discuss strategies for handling similar situations in the future.
- ❏ Role-play different scenarios where your child may need to say 'no' and brainstorm confident ways to respond.
- ❏ Encourage mindfulness techniques, such as deep breathing or counting to ten before reacting to stressful situations.

Thank you for reinforcing these important skills at home.

✂ -------------------------------------- ✂   CUT HERE

Session 4: Mindful of Me: Self-Control/Peer Pressure

Dear Parent/Guardian,

Today's *Brotherhood* small group session focused on self-control and handling peer pressure. The boys participated in activities that helped them recognize the power of their choices and how to resist negative influences. They also discussed ways to remain true to themselves in challenging situations.

How you can reinforce this at home:

- ❏ Talk to your child about a time when they faced peer pressure and discuss strategies for handling similar situations in the future.
- ❏ Role-play different scenarios where your child may need to say 'no' and brainstorm confident ways to respond.
- ❏ Encourage mindfulness techniques, such as deep breathing or counting to ten before reacting to stressful situations.

Thank you for reinforcing these important skills at home.

My Choice, My Responsibility

Making Choices/Accountability

DOI: 10.4324/9781003410409-6

SESSION 5: MY CHOICE, MY RESPONSIBILITY

Making Choices/Accountability

Student Learning Outcomes
❑ Students will understand the difference between accountability (ownership of actions) and responsibility (task-related obligations).
❑ Students will analyze scenarios to identify possible choices and their corresponding consequences.
❑ Through role-play, students will model positive and negative choices and the associated consequences.
❑ Students will discuss and reflect on how accountability and responsibility impact personal growth and future success.

Materials Needed
❑ Whiteboard or chart paper (*to write 'Accountability vs. Responsibility' and key definitions*)
❑ Markers, pens, pencils
❑ Notebook paper or journals (*for students to take notes or write down thoughts during the warm-up questions*)
❑ Choice cards (*pre-made cards with various scenarios related to choices and consequences; enough for each group of 3–4 students*)
❑ Role-play planning sheets (*worksheets for students to outline their positive/negative choices and consequences for their assigned scenarios*)
❑ Index cards or small notebooks (*for students to jot down lines or ideas for their role-plays*)
❑ Discussion questions
❑ Check for Understanding: script templates

Worksheets Included
❑ Session 5: Choice Cards
❑ Session 5: Check for Understanding
❑ Session 5: Parent/Guardian Letter

Session 5: Lesson Plan

Do Now (Warm-Up)

Start by writing the words 'Accountability vs. Responsibility'. Ask students if they know the difference between the two. Share with students:

- ❏ Responsibility is about the actions you are supposed to take if given a task or duty.
- ❏ Accountability is about taking ownership of your actions and choices.

Give the example: Your teacher instructs you to create a detailed study guide for a test tomorrow. You are **responsible** for creating this study guide and ensuring that you bring it to class tomorrow for the test. If you forget the study guide or decide not to complete it, you will need to take **accountability** for not being prepared for the test (and potentially not passing).

Ask students: Why is it important that we make positive choices?

Ask students: What are some potential consequences if we make negative choices?

Activity

Explain to students that they are going to participate in a choice-and-consequence role-play activity. Divide students into groups of 3 or 4 students.

Each group will receive a choice card with a scenario. On their choice cards, they will need to do the following:

1. Create a positive and negative choice for the scenario.
2. Create a corresponding positive and negative consequence for each of the positive and negative choices they created.
3. Have each group choose which action they would take and the corresponding consequence.
4. Have students create a mini role-play of the choice and consequence they select from their scenario (should be 3–5 minutes in length).
5. Students should share their mini role-plays with the whole group.

Let's Talk About It (Discussion)

Facilitate group discussion using the following questions:
- ❏ How did it feel to create positive and negative choices for your scenario?
- ❏ Why is it important to think about the outcomes/consequences for all your choices?
- ❏ What are things that impact us when we are thinking about making a positive or negative choice?
- ❏ Provide examples of how a negative choice could impact your future.
- ❏ When our responsibility is to make positive choices but we make a negative choice, why is it important that we take accountability for the choice we made?

CHECK FOR UNDERSTANDING

'Explain it to a Friend': Have students create a script outlining how they would explain today's lesson to their peers.

Session 5: Choice Cards

Scenario: Turning in Homework You forgot to complete your math homework last night and the teacher asks you to hand it in as you arrive in the classroom. 1. Create a positive choice and a positive consequence. 2. Create a negative choice and a negative consequence. 3. Prepare a mini role-play skit of your scenario and include one of the choices/consequences (positive choice/positive consequence; negative choice/negative consequence).	**Scenario: Helping a Friend** Your friend asks you for help on an assignment, but you also have your own work to finish. 1. Create a positive choice and a positive consequence. 2. Create a negative choice and a negative consequence. 3. Prepare a mini role-play skit of your scenario and include one of the choices/consequences (positive choice/positive consequence; negative choice/negative consequence).
Scenario: Taking Responsibility Your parent(s) asked you to clean your room before going out to play, but your friends want you to go out and play now. Your parent(s) are at work. 1. Create a positive choice and a positive consequence. 2. Create a negative choice and a negative consequence. 3. Prepare a mini role-play skit of your scenario and include one of the choices/consequences (positive choice/positive consequence; negative choice/negative consequence).	**Scenario: Being Honest** You accidentally broke a classroom supply that the teacher said was very important. No one saw you break it. 1. Create a positive choice and a positive consequence. 2. Create a negative choice and a negative consequence. 3. Prepare a mini role-play skit of your scenario and include one of the choices/consequences (positive choice/positive consequence; negative choice/negative consequence).

Scenario: Standing Up to Peer Pressure Your friends ask you to skip class and hang out during lunch. They tell you that they never get caught, but you feel you will get caught as your teacher takes attendance. 1. Create a positive choice and a positive consequence. 2. Create a negative choice and a negative consequence. 3. Prepare a mini role-play skit of your scenario and include one of the choices/consequences (positive choice/positive consequence; negative choice/negative consequence).	**Scenario: Completing a Group Project** You're working on a group project but one of your teammates isn't doing their part. The project is due tomorrow. 1. Create a positive choice and a positive consequence. 2. Create a negative choice and a negative consequence. 3. Prepare a mini role-play skit of your scenario and include one of the choices/consequences (positive choice/positive consequence; negative choice/negative consequence).
Scenario: Using Time Wisely You have a test tomorrow, but your friend has challenged you in a virtual video game competition tonight. 1. Create a positive choice and a positive consequence. 2. Create a negative choice and a negative consequence. 3. Prepare a mini role-play skit of your scenario and include one of the choices/consequences (positive choice/positive consequence; negative choice/negative consequence).	**Scenario: Being a Leader** During a school project, your group starts arguing about how to get started. You notice the group isn't making any progress. 1. Create a positive choice and a positive consequence. 2. Create a negative choice and a negative consequence. 3. Prepare a mini role-play skit of your scenario and include one of the choices/consequences (positive choice/positive consequence; negative choice/negative consequence).

Session 5: Check for Understanding Worksheet

'Explain it to a Friend'

Pretend you are asked to explain what you learned today to a friend. Write a script outlining what you learned today with a friend. Be sure to include the following:

- ❏ The difference between responsibility and accountability.
- ❏ The importance of making positive decisions.
- ❏ The importance of considering consequences when making decisions.

Session 5: My Choice, My Responsibility: Decision-Making & Accountability

Dear Parent/Guardian,

In today's *Brotherhood* small group, we explored the importance of making responsible choices and taking ownership of our actions. The boys analyzed different scenarios to understand the consequences of their decisions and practiced role-playing both positive and negative choices.

How you can reinforce this at home:

❏ Ask your child about a scenario they discussed today and how they would handle it differently now.
❏ Help them think through decisions by asking, 'What might happen if you choose this?'
❏ Model accountability by acknowledging mistakes and discussing how to make things right.

Your support makes a difference in shaping responsible young men.

✂ -- ✂ CUT HERE

Session 5: My Choice, My Responsibility: Decision-Making & Accountability

Dear Parent/Guardian,

In today's *Brotherhood* small group, we explored the importance of making responsible choices and taking ownership of our actions. The boys analyzed different scenarios to understand the consequences of their decisions and practiced role-playing both positive and negative choices.

How you can reinforce this at home:

❏ Ask your child about a scenario they discussed today and how they would handle it differently now.
❏ Help them think through decisions by asking, 'What might happen if you choose this?'
❏ Model accountability by acknowledging mistakes and discussing how to make things right.

Your support makes a difference in shaping responsible young men.

Not Me, But We

*Teamwork/Sportsmanship/
Brotherhood*

DOI: 10.4324/9781003410409-7

SESSION 6: NOT ME, BUT WE

Teamwork/Sportsmanship/Brotherhood

Student Learning Outcomes
❑ Students will demonstrate effective teamwork skills by collaborating and strategizing with their group to complete the 'Cross the River' challenge.
❑ Students will practice communication and non-verbal problem solving by planning their approach and following silent cues during the activity.
❑ Students will demonstrate sportsmanship by encouraging their teammates throughout the activity and by showing respect to all participants, including congratulating the other team after the challenge.
❑ Students will reflect on the importance of teamwork and sportsmanship by identifying **3** things they learned about teamwork, **2** ways to show good sportsmanship, and **1** way to be a supportive teammate on the 3-2-1 reflection worksheet.

Materials Needed
❑ Lily pads (*use items like foam circles, poly spots, or pieces of cardboard to represent lily pads; you'll need about five lily pads per team – or adjust based on the distance across the 'river'*)
❑ Timer
❑ Boundary maker (*use cones or tape to outline the 'river' edges and designate starting and finishing points*)
❑ Markers
❑ 3-2-1 reflection sheets
❑ Pencils/pens

Worksheets Included
❑ Session 6: Do Now Worksheet
❑ Session 6: Check for Understanding
❑ Session 6: Parent/Guardian Letter

Session 6: Lesson Plan

Do Now (Warm-Up)

Using the 'Do Now' worksheet or their journals, students should write down **three** positive traits of a teammate and **three** negative traits of a teammate.

Activity

Students will be divided into two equal teams (if teams are unequal, one student will need to go twice). Students are to 'cross the river' without falling into the water. The first team that ensures all its members cross the river without falling into the water will win.

Provide students with 'lily pads' to get across the river. (The number of lily pads should be determined by the distance from one side of the river to the other. Typically, five lily pads are effective and still provide a challenge for students.)

Share the following instructions with students:
1. The purpose of this activity is to work as a team. Teams will have a few minutes to strategize and create a plan to ensure that all its members cross the river without falling into the water.
2. Once the timer begins, you will not be able to verbally communicate with teammates once they begin crossing the river. *Note*: While onshore, you are able to communicate with other team members who are also on the shore.
3. You may utilize the lily pads you were given to cross the river.
4. Once a team member has crossed the river they should encourage and cheer other teammates on.
5. When all teammates have crossed, all teammates should raise their right hand to signify that they have completed the challenge.

Rules
1. No talking while you are crossing the river.
2. If you step/fall into the river, you are out and have to start over.
3. You may only utilize the lily pads to cross the river.
4. All team members must cross the river before the team can raise their right hands.
5. First team to cross the river with all its members wins the challenge.

After the challenge is over and a winner has been declared, have all the students shake hands or high-five each other.

Let's Talk About It (Discussion)

- ❏ What was it like to have to plan and strategize with your team?
- ❏ How did it feel to have your teammates cheer you on as you crossed the river?
- ❏ How did it feel to be a listener only as you are crossing the river?
- ❏ Why do you think teamwork is important?
- ❏ What do you think it means when they say 'Teamwork makes the dreamwork?'
- ❏ Why do you think you were instructed to shake hands after the game?
- ❏ What is good sportsmanship?

CHECK FOR UNDERSTANDING

3-2-1: Have students complete the 3-2-1 on a reflection sheet to go into their folders or in their notebook journals.

- ❏ **3** things you learned about working in a team.
- ❏ **2** ways you can show good sportsmanship.
- ❏ **1** thing you think you can do to be a good teammate.

Session 6: Do Now Worksheet

Complete the chart by writing down 3 positive traits/characteristics of a teammate and 3 negative traits/characteristics of a teammate.

Positive Traits	Negative Traits
1.	1.
2.	2.
3.	3.

Session 6: Check for Understanding Worksheet

3-2-1

Answer the following questions:

- ❏ **3** things you learned about working in a team.
- ❏ **2** ways you can show good sportsmanship.
- ❏ **1** thing you think you can do to be a good teammate.

Session 6: Not Me, But We: Teamwork, Sportsmanship, and Brotherhood

Dear Parent/Guardian,

Today's *Brotherhood* small group session was all about teamwork and sportsmanship. The boys worked together to complete a 'Cross the River' challenge, which required communication, strategy, and collaboration. They also discussed the importance of being a good teammate and showing sportsmanship, both in and out of competition.

How you can reinforce this at home:

- ❏ Ask your child how their team worked together to complete the challenge and what strategies they used.
- ❏ Encourage them to think about ways they can be a supportive teammate at home, in school, or during sports.
- ❏ Discuss what good sportsmanship looks like—celebrating others' success, handling loss gracefully, and encouraging peers.

Thank you for encouraging a spirit of teamwork in your child.

Session 6: Not Me, But We: Teamwork, Sportsmanship, and Brotherhood

Dear Parent/Guardian,

Today's *Brotherhood* small group session was all about teamwork and sportsmanship. The boys worked together to complete a 'Cross the River' challenge, which required communication, strategy, and collaboration. They also discussed the importance of being a good teammate and showing sportsmanship, both in and out of competition.

How you can reinforce this at home:

- ❏ Ask your child how their team worked together to complete the challenge and what strategies they used.
- ❏ Encourage them to think about ways they can be a supportive teammate at home, in school, or during sports.
- ❏ Discuss what good sportsmanship looks like—celebrating others' success, handling loss gracefully, and encouraging peers.

Thank you for encouraging a spirit of teamwork in your child.

Lead the Way

Leadership & Service

DOI: 10.4324/9781003410409-8

SESSION 7: LEAD THE WAY

Leadership & Service

Student Learning Outcomes
❑ Students will define leadership and identify key characteristics/traits of effective leaders.
❑ Students will collaborate with peers to demonstrate leadership traits through role-play.
❑ Students will analyze and evaluate leadership behaviors through observation and discussion.
❑ Students will set actionable goals to enhance their leadership abilities.
Materials Needed
❑ Bulletin paper/whiteboard and markers
❑ Index cards (*for writing leadership characteristics/traits*)
❑ Timer/online stopwatch
❑ Student notebook journals/folders (*for 'Do Now' and 'Check for Understanding' assignments*)
Worksheets Included
❑ Session 7: Do Now Worksheet
❑ Session 7: Check for Understanding
❑ Session 7: Parent/Guardian Letter

Session 7: Lesson Plan

Do Now (Warm-Up)

Have students write about how they believe they have shown leadership. Ask them to share their responses with the group and discuss the following prompts:

- ❏ What does it mean to be a leader?
- ❏ How did they know they were serving/acting as a leader?
- ❏ What made them want to lead?
- ❏ What are some characteristics/traits that leaders must have? If students (and facilitator) agree on these characteristics/traits, write them on bulletin paper or a whiteboard (for all to see) and also individually on index cards for the activity.

Activity

Divide the students into small groups with three to four in each group. Each group will choose one index card from the 'Do Now' activity. The index card will indicate which characteristic or trait the group will demonstrate through role-play.

The activity will be as follows:

1. Each group will have 15 minutes to prepare a short role-play or skit that will demonstrate what their chosen characteristic will look like.

   Example: Students' index card reads 'Team Player'. The group will showcase a student leader exemplifying a leader being a team player.

2. Each characteristic/trait will be displayed on the board so students who are observing the role-play have a 'word bank' to choose from.

3. Other groups who observe the role-play will share which characteristic/trait they feel the group displayed in the role-play.

Let's Talk About It (Discussion):

After all groups have presented their role-plays and observers have identified characteristics/traits, have the students come together to discuss.

Utilize the following prompts to guide discussion:
- ❏ What were some specific things that you saw in the role-plays that you liked?
- ❏ Why is it important to be a good and effective leader?
- ❏ What would you describe as your 'superpower' leadership skill? (What is your leadership strength?)

CHECK FOR UNDERSTANDING

3-2-1: Have students complete the 3-2-1 on a reflection sheet to go into their folders or in their notebook journals.

- ❏ List **3** characteristics/traits of an effective leader.
- ❏ What are **2** ways you will work to be an effective leader?
- ❏ What is **1** way you can show leadership this week?

Preparing for the Next Group Session

Share with students that the next group session will be preparation for their finale presentation (or whatever you/the students have decided). Contingent upon what you decide for your culminating/end-of-group activity, prepare and inform students of what they will need to bring, if anything, and the ways they will need to prepare. Feel free to use this as additional planning space and for reminders.

Session 7: Do Now Worksheet

Write about how you feel you have shown leadership.

Here are some examples: babysitting, captain of an athletic team, line leader, hall or cafeteria monitor, etc.

Session 7: Check for Understanding Worksheet

3-2-1

Answer the following:

- ❏ List **3** characteristics/traits of an effective leader.
- ❏ What are **2** ways you will work to be an effective leader?
- ❏ What is **1** way you can show leadership this week?

Session 7: Lead the Way: Leadership & Service

Dear Parent/Guardian,

In today's *Brotherhood* small group session, we focused on leadership. The boys explored the characteristics of strong leaders and engaged in role-playing activities to demonstrate leadership in action. They also identified their personal leadership strengths and how they can use them in their everyday lives.

How you can reinforce this at home:

- ❏ Ask your child what leadership traits they demonstrated in today's activity.
- ❏ Encourage them to take on small leadership roles at home, such as helping a younger sibling, setting the table, or organizing a family activity.
- ❏ Share examples of leaders in your family or community and discuss what makes them effective.

Your support in developing leadership skills will help your child become a strong, confident leader.

✂ – ✂   CUT HERE

Session 7: Lead the Way: Leadership & Service

Dear Parent/Guardian,

In today's *Brotherhood* small group session, we focused on leadership. The boys explored the characteristics of strong leaders and engaged in role-playing activities to demonstrate leadership in action. They also identified their personal leadership strengths and how they can use them in their everyday lives.

How you can reinforce this at home:

- ❏ Ask your child what leadership traits they demonstrated in today's activity.
- ❏ Encourage them to take on small leadership roles at home, such as helping a younger sibling, setting the table, or organizing a family activity.
- ❏ Share examples of leaders in your family or community and discuss what makes them effective.

Your support in developing leadership skills will help your child become a strong, confident leader.

Brotherhood Member Presentation Finale

Preparation

DOI: 10.4324/9781003410409-9

SESSION 8: BROTHERHOOD MEMBER PRESENTATION PREPARATION

Background

This is a special time for boys in the group. Today's session will focus on preparing for the group finale. This session serves as an example of a culminating activity. It can be modified or re-created with an activity of your own or an activity of what the group decides. Alternative group finale ideas follow this lesson plan.

Brotherhood Group Presentation Finale (BGPF)

The group finale presentation is a 'Brotherhood Member Presentation'. It will showcase the boys' vision boards (goals), their final take away from group, and recitation of the Brotherhood Oath which will indicate their induction into the school's Brotherhood. This presentation is an hour-long (or a little less) program that takes place typically during the day, usually during a lunch period. Parents and teachers of the participants, school staff, and administrators are invited to attend. Important documents and items pertaining to the BGPF can be found following this lesson plan.

Session 8: Overview

The boys will utilize this entire session to prepare for the finale and complete the post-test survey.

Student Learning Outcomes
❏ Students will reflect on their personal growth and experiences in the group through creative and written expression.
❏ Students will articulate their goals and the steps needed to achieve them through a vision board activity.
❏ Students will express their reflections on the group experience through journaling..
Materials Needed
Vision Board:
❏ Post-test survey (*page 89*)
❏ Invitations for Brotherhood Membership Presentation (*sample email on page 82*)
❏ Brotherhood Oath index card
❏ Student notebook journals/folders
Vision Board:
❏ Poster board or large paper
❏ Markers, crayons, colored pencils
❏ Magazines/stickers (*for pictures/words*)
Worksheets Included
❏ Session 8: Check for Understanding
❏ Session 8: Parent/Guardian Letter

Session 8: Lesson Plan

Do Now (Warm-Up)

Students will complete the post-test survey.

Activity

Step 1
Students will creatively write/draw/decorate their vision board with the following:

- ❏ I am (**Participant's Name**) and I am (**adjective that describes participant**).
  - ■ *Example adjectives*: amazing, cool, creative, intelligent, athletic, etc.
- ❏ When I grow up, I am going to be a(n) _____
  - ■ *Examples*: doctor, pilot, architect, engineer, athlete, etc.
- ❏ To achieve this goal, I am going to _____
  _____ (list **three** things that you will need to do to achieve *your goal*).
  - ■ *Examples*: study often, practice daily, attend school everyday, complete my homework.

Step 2
Practice the Brotherhood Oath in the way it will be presented at the membership presentation. Participants can commit the oath to memory or read the oath from an index card or prompt on the wall. Participants can also read/recite parts of the oath in groups of two or three.

Brotherhood Group Oath

I am (Student's name _____)

I am strong, courageous, and intelligent.
I am my brother's keeper!
I lead with integrity and empathy.
I celebrate who I am and where I am from.
I always strive for excellence.

Let's Discuss

Have a conversation regarding what the finale presentation will look like and answer any questions students may have. Practicing the Oath and sharing their final journal entry may be helpful as well.

CHECK FOR UNDERSTANDING

Students will write one last journal entry to share aloud at the presentation.

Journal Prompt: In two to three sentences, write about what you have learned in the Boys Group or how you feel you are different because of this group.

Session 8: Check for Understanding

Journal Prompt

In two to three sentences, write about what you have learned in the Boys Group or how you feel you are different because of this group. Feel free to use both words and images for creative expression.

Session 8: Brotherhood Member Presentation Preparation

Dear Parent/Guardian,

As we approach the *Brotherhood* group finale, today's session focused on reflecting on the journey so far. The boys worked on vision boards to showcase their goals, practiced the *Brotherhood Oath*, and prepared for their final presentation. This session was an opportunity for them to recognize their growth, set future goals, and celebrate their accomplishments.

How you can reinforce this at home:

- ❏ Ask your child to share their vision board and explain the goals they set for themselves.
- ❏ Practice the *Brotherhood Oath* together and discuss what it means to them.
- ❏ Celebrate their hard work in *Brotherhood* small group by acknowledging their growth and encouraging them to continue striving for success.

We look forward to seeing you at the upcoming *Brotherhood* small group Membership Presentation to celebrate your child's journey.

Brotherhood Member Presentation Finale

Materials

DOI: 10.4324/9781003410409-10

Email Invitation to Teachers, Staff, and Administrators

Greetings Teachers, Administrators, & Staff,

We are thrilled to invite you to join us in celebrating the achievements and growth of our Brotherhood Small Group participants during their Membership Presentation Finale.

This special event marks the culmination of weeks of hard work, personal development, and leadership growth for the young men in the group. The presentation will showcase their journey, highlight the skills they've developed, and honor their commitment to becoming young men and future leaders.

Brotherhood Membership Presentation Details

Date: _____

Time: _____

Location: _____

If you have any questions, please feel free to reach out to _____ _____ [*School Counselor name/email*].

We look forward to seeing you at the Brotherhood Membership Presentation.

_____
[*School Counselor name*]

Invitation Letter to Parents

Dear Parent/Guardian,

We are thrilled to invite you to the Brotherhood Membership Presentation Finale, a special event celebrating the growth, achievements, and hard work of the boys who participated in the Brotherhood Small Group Counseling Program.

Brotherhood Membership Presentation Details

Date: _____

Time: _____

Location: _____

The Brotherhood Membership Presentation Finale marks the culmination of a meaningful journey for these young men. Over the course of the program, they have explored leadership, accountability, and teamwork while developing the tools to succeed academically, socially, and emotionally. This event will showcase their reflections, growth, and the powerful bond they have formed as a group.

Highlights of the event will include:

- ❏ A presentation of the Brotherhood Oath
- ❏ Sharing of vision boards and personal reflections
- ❏ Recognition of each participant's achievements

We would be honored to have you join us as we celebrate your child's journey and commitment to becoming a leader and role model. Your presence will mean so much to your child and the entire Brotherhood Group.

Please RSVP by _____ [insert RSVP date] to _____ [School Counselor's name] via email at _____ [School Counselor's email] or via phone _____ [School Counselor's phone number].

Thank you for your continued support. We look forward to celebrating this special milestone with you.

Warm regards,

_____ [School Counselor's name]

Sample Program

Brotherhood Membership Presentation Finale

_____ [*School name*]

Welcome _____ School Counselor

About Brotherhood _____ Desired Participant

Goal Presentations _____ All Participants

Brotherhood Oath _____ All Participants

Presentation of Membership Certificates _____
Administration and School Counselor

Thank you for supporting our boys! We hope you enjoyed the program!

Refreshments Served

Brotherhood Oath Cut-Outs

These can be cut (and laminated) for students to have.

Brotherhood Oath I am – – – – – – – – – – – – – – – – – – – I am strong, courageous, and intelligent. I am my brother's keeper! I lead with integrity and empathy. I celebrate who I am and where I am from. I always strive for excellence.	**Brotherhood Oath** I am – – – – – – – – – – – – – – – – – – – I am strong, courageous, and intelligent. I am my brother's keeper! I lead with integrity and empathy. I celebrate who I am and where I am from. I always strive for excellence.
Brotherhood Oath I am – – – – – – – – – – – – – – – – – – – I am strong, courageous, and intelligent. I am my brother's keeper! I lead with integrity and empathy. I celebrate who I am and where I am from. I always strive for excellence.	**Brotherhood Oath** I am – – – – – – – – – – – – – – – – – – – I am strong, courageous, and intelligent. I am my brother's keeper! I lead with integrity and empathy. I celebrate who I am and where I am from. I always strive for excellence.

Brotherhood Certificate of Membership

Certificate of Membership

This certificate certifies that

_____

**is an official member of the
Brotherhood Group**

_____

School Counselor

_____

School Administrator

Date _____

Appendix A
Program Evaluation Tools

Brotherhood Pre-Group Survey

Instructions: Answer the following questions honestly. There are no right or wrong answers. Your answers will help in understanding how to better support you during the group sessions.

1. What is a leader?	
2. How confident are you in your leadership skills?	❏ 1 Not confident at all ❏ 2 Somewhat confident ❏ 3 Confident ❏ 4 Really confident
3. I know how to handle challenges like peer pressure or bullying.	❏ True ❏ False ❏ Somewhat/Unsure
4. What does accountability mean to you?	❏ Taking responsibility for your actions ❏ Blaming others when things go wrong ❏ Avoiding responsibility ❏ I am unsure
5. How do you feel about your heritage and background?	❏ Not proud ❏ Somewhat proud ❏ Very proud ❏ Unsure
6. Do you have any goals for yourself this year?	❏ Yes ❏ No
7. If 'yes', you have goals for yourself, what are they?	
8. What does it mean to be a team player?	
9. How well do you believe you work in a team?	❏ I do not work well with others in a team. ❏ I work okay with others in a team. ❏ I work well with others in a team. ❏ I am unsure how I work with others in a team.
10. How comfortable are you speaking in front of others?	❏ Not comfortable ❏ Somewhat comfortable ❏ Comfortable ❏ Very comfortable

Brotherhood Post-Group Survey

Instructions: Answer the following questions honestly. There are no right or wrong answers. Your answers will help in understanding how to better support you during the group sessions.

1. What is a leader?	
2. How confident are you in your leadership skills now?	❏ 1 Not confident at all ❏ 2 Somewhat confident ❏ 3 Confident ❏ 4 Really confident
3. I know how to handle challenges like peer pressure or bullying.	❏ True ❏ False ❏ Somewhat/Unsure
4. What does accountability mean to you now?	❏ Taking responsibility for your actions ❏ Blaming others when things go wrong ❏ Avoiding responsibility ❏ I am unsure
5. How do you feel about your heritage and background now?	❏ Not proud ❏ Somewhat proud ❏ Very proud ❏ Unsure
6. What are the goals you have for yourself?	
7. What does it mean to be a team player?	
8. How well do you believe you work in a team?	❏ I do not work well with others in a team. ❏ I work okay with others in a team. ❏ I work well with others in a team. ❏ I am unsure how I work with others in a team.
9. How comfortable are you speaking in front of others now?	❏ Not comfortable ❏ Somewhat comfortable ❏ Comfortable ❏ Very comfortable

Brotherhood Pre-Group Teacher Evaluation

Instructions: Your feedback will help us identify the needs of students participating in the Brotherhood Group. Please answer the following questions based on your observations.

1. Do you think the student you are referring to the Brotherhood demonstrates leadership potential?	❏ Yes ❏ Somewhat ❏ No
2. How confident is this student in expressing their ideas?	❏ Very confident ❏ Somewhat confident ❏ Neutral ❏ Not confident
3. How does this student handle challenges such as peer pressure or bullying?	❏ Effectively ❏ Somewhat effectively ❏ Ineffectively ❏ I'm not sure
4. Does this student show accountability for their actions?	❏ Often ❏ Sometimes ❏ Rarely ❏ Never
5. How would you rate the students' behavior on a scale from 1 to 5? *1 – need improvement; 5 – model student*	❏ 1 ❏ 2 ❏ 3 ❏ 4 ❏ 5
6. What strengths does this student demonstrate in social or academic settings?	
7. What challenges do you think this student would benefit from addressing in the group?	

Brotherhood Post-Group Teacher Evaluation

Instructions: Your feedback will help us identify the needs of students partici-pating in the Brotherhood Group. Please answer the following questions based on your observations.

1. Do you think the student you are referring to the Brotherhood demonstrates leadership potential now?	❏ Yes ❏ Somewhat ❏ No
2. How confident is this student in expressing their ideas now?	❏ Very confident ❏ Somewhat confident ❏ Neutral ❏ Not confident
3. How does this student handle challenges such as peer pressure or bullying now?	❏ Effectively ❏ Somewhat effectively ❏ Ineffectively ❏ I'm not sure
4. Does this student show accountability for their actions now?	❏ Often ❏ Sometimes ❏ Rarely ❏ Never
5. How would you rate the students' behavior on a scale from 1 to 5 now? 1 – *need improvement*; 5 – *model student*	❏ 1 ❏ 2 ❏ 3 ❏ 4 ❏ 5
6. What strengths have you observed from this student in social or academic settings post-group?	
7. What areas of growth do you observe are still needed for this student?	

Brotherhood Post-Group Parent Evaluation

Thank you for allowing your student to be a part of the Brotherhood Small Group Counseling Program. Please take a few moments to share feedback regarding any changes you may have seen in your child as a result of participating in the Brotherhood group.

1. How would you rate your overall satisfaction with the Brotherhood Group?	a. Very satisfied b. Satisfied c. Neutral d. Dissatisfied e. Very satisfied
2. Do you feel the program met its goals of supporting your child's social, emotional and leadership development?	a. Strongly agree b. Agree c. Neutral d. Disagree e. Strongly disagree
3. Do you feel your child benefited from participating in the program?	a. Yes, significantly b. Yes, somewhat c. Neutral d. Not much
4. What changes, if any, have you noticed in your child since participating in the group?	a. Increased confidence b. Improved communication skills c. Greater sense of responsibility and accountability d. Stronger leadership skills e. Pride in heritage and self-identity
5. What did your child share with you about their experience in the Brotherhood group?	
6. Do you feel the program addressed challenges your child may face, such as peer pressure or bullying?	a. Yes, very well b. Somewhat c. Neutral d. Not much e. Not at all

Program Structure

7. How would you rate the communication and updates you received about the program?	a. Excellent b. Good c. Neutral d. Poor e. Very poor
8. Were the program goals and activities clearly explained to you?	a. Yes b. Somewhat c. No
9. What suggestions, if any, do you have for improving the program?	
10. Would you recommend the Brotherhood Small Group Counseling Program to other parents?	a. Yes b. No c. Unsure

Appendix B
Tracking Forms

Brotherhood Minute Meeting Tracker

Utilize this minute meeting tracker to meet with potential participants for the group or utilize to meet with participants throughout the group.

Student Name	Date	Quick Notes

Brotherhood Attendance Tracker

Student Name	Week 1	Week 2	Week 3	Week 4	Week 5	Week 6	Week 7	Week 8

Brotherhood Data Tracker

Individual Student Growth

Student Name	Pre-Test	Post Test	Growth Notes

Brotherhood Data Tracker

Overall Group Growth

Use this data tracker to track the overall student growth of your group based on the key student learning objective areas.

Area of Growth	Pre-Test	Post-Test	Teacher Feedback	Parent Feedback	Journal Notes/ Feedback
Brotherhood					
Goal Setting					
Self-Esteem					
Self-Control/Peer Pressure					
Making Choices					
Relationships/ Teamwork					
Communication					
Leadership					
Presentation Skills/Public Speaking					

Brotherhood Group Member Follow-Up

Note: The group member follow-up can be a written assignment (paper or electronic) or it can be done as a brief individual counseling session.

WOW! Can you believe that it has been _____ month(s) since we have met as a group? It's important to check in with you and see how things are going.

Please complete this sheet and return it to _____ office.

Student Name: _____	Date: _____
1. What do you remember from our group?	
2. Have you been working on your goals? If so, in what ways?	
3. Have you achieved any of the goals you set in the group?	
4. Were you able to make any friends from the group? If so, who?	
5. What did you learn most from the group?	
6. What was your favorite part of the group?	
7. What was your least favorite part of the group	
8. What are you doing differently because of your time in the group?	

Appendix C
Quick Session Reference Preparation Guide

Session 1: Brotherhood

Student Learning Outcomes
❑ Students will identify and establish key group norms for successful collaboration and respect within the group.
❑ Students will develop trust-building skills by participating in a guided obstacle course activity.
❑ Students will reflect on their role as both a listener and a communicator, identifying personal areas for improvement.

Materials Needed
❑ Folders or notebooks (*for storing worksheets, journal entries, handouts*)
❑ Brotherhood Oath document (*for students to sign*)
❑ Group member pre-test (*for assessment*)
❑ Poster paper or large paper (*to write down group norms*)
❑ Markers (*for writing norms on poster paper*)
❑ Blindfolds (*for trust-building obstacle course activity*)
❑ Desks/chairs/cones (*for setting up the obstacle course*)
❑ 3-2-1 Reflection Sheets or Written on Board/Poster (*for reflection and checks for understanding*)

Session 2: Ready, Set, Mindset: Setting Goals & Academic Excellence

Student Learning Outcomes
❏ Students will develop SMART goals for both academic and personal growth.   ❏ Students will identify strengths and resources that can help them achieve their goals.   ❏ Students will predict and analyze any potential obstacles that might impact them as they are working towards their goals   ❏ Students will develop problem-solving skills to best navigate challenges and obstacles that may prevent them from achieving their goals.
Materials Needed

❏ 5 large poster boards or easels (*for each checkpoint station*):
   ■ Label each board with the specific checkpoint and instructions:
     ○ Checkpoint 1: SMART goals (Create one academic and one personal goal)
     ○ Checkpoint 2: Strengths and resources
     ○ Checkpoint 3: Obstacles and challenges
     ○ Checkpoint 4: Strategies to overcome challenges
     ○ Checkpoint 5: Rewrite and commit to your goal
 ❏ Pens/pencils (*enough for all students*)
 ❏ Student journals/notebooks or loose-leaf paper
 ❏ SMART goals practice worksheets
 ❏ Music playlist (*optional, playing softly in the background to set the mood*)
 	
 Checkpoint station materials:
 	
 ❏ Checkpoint 1 (SMART goals):
   ■ Printed SMART goal templates (*enough for each student*)
 ❏ Checkpoint 2 (Strengths and resources):
   ■ Strength and resource identification sheets (a *simple worksheet with prompts to list their strengths and resources*)
 ❏ Checkpoint 3 (Obstacles and challenges):
   ■ Obstacle identification sheets (*for students to write down challenges they foresee*)
 ❏ Checkpoint 4 (Strategies to overcome challenges):
   ■ Strategy development sheets (*for brainstorming ways to overcome obstacles*)
 ❏ Checkpoint 5 (Mountain peak/overlook):
   ■ Final goal sheet templates (*clean and aesthetically pleasing templates for students to rewrite their goals and sign them*)
   ■ Frames or construction paper (*optional, for students to 'frame' their goals and display them*)

Session 3: I am Me!
Self-Identity & Confidence

Student Learning Outcomes
❏ Students will understand the importance of authenticity and self-acceptance.
❏ Students will identify and express personal strengths, values, and challenges.
❏ Students will demonstrate creativity in expressing their identity.
❏ Students will engage in meaningful group discussions and provide positive feedback to peers.

Materials Needed
❏ Classroom desks/tables (*for students to rest their heads and cover their eyes*)
❏ Facilitator's statement sheet (*list of statements for the heads-up activity*)
❏ 'Shield of _____' Worksheets (*enough for each student, pre-printed*)
❏ Pens, pencils, crayons/colored pencils, markers
❏ Discussion prompts (*prepared in advance, can be written on the board or printed as a handout*)
❏ Reflection sheets (*3-2-1 format, enough for each student, or students can use their notebooks*)

Session 4: Mindful of Me: Self-Control/Peer Pressure

Student Learning Outcomes
❏ Students will define peer pressure and identify examples of both positive and negative peer influences.
❏ Students will practice resisting peer pressure through role-play scenarios and understanding the consequences of their choices.
❏ Students will explore self-control techniques for managing emotions and impulses when experiencing peer pressure.
❏ Students will reflect on past experiences with peer pressure and develop strategies for making better decisions in the future.

Materials Needed
❏ Sticky notes (*one per student*)
❏ Markers or pens
❏ Poster boards or large paper labeled 'Positive Pressure/Influence' and 'Negative Pressure/Influence'
❏ Tug of War rope (*with a marked center point or ribbon to indicate the boundary*)
❏ Floor markers (*to mark the boundary line on the floor*)
❏ Index cards with peer pressure scenarios for each round:
■ Round 1 Scenario: Teasing for breaking rules
■ Round 2 Scenario: Cheating on a test
■ Round 3 Scenario: Fighting due to disrespect
❏ Journals or notebooks or loose paper if students are using personal folders
❏ Pens or pencils for writing
❏ Check for Understanding Worksheet

Session 5: My Choice, My Responsibility: Making Choices/Accountability

Student Learning Outcomes
❑ Students will understand the difference between accountability (ownership of actions) and responsibility (task-related obligations).
❑ Students will analyze scenarios to identify possible choices and their corresponding consequences.
❑ Through role-play, students will model positive and negative choices and the associated consequences.
❑ Students will discuss and reflect on how accountability and responsibility impact personal growth and future success.

Materials Needed
❑ Whiteboard or chart paper (*to write 'Accountability vs. Responsibility' and key definitions*)
❑ Markers, pens, pencils
❑ Notebook paper or journals (*for students to take notes or write down thoughts during the warm-up questions*)
❑ Choice cards (*pre-made cards with various scenarios related to choices and consequences; enough for each group of 3–4 students*)
❑ Role-play planning sheets (*worksheets for students to outline their positive/ negative choices and consequences for their assigned scenarios*)
❑ Index cards or small notebooks (*for students to jot down lines or ideas for their role-plays*)
❑ Discussion questions
❑ Check for Understanding: script templates

Session 6: Not Me, But We: Teamwork/Sportsmanship/Brotherhood

Student Learning Outcomes
❏ Students will demonstrate effective teamwork skills by collaborating and strategizing with their group to complete the 'Cross the River' challenge.
❏ Students will practice communication and non-verbal problem solving by planning their approach and following silent cues during the activity.
❏ Students will demonstrate sportsmanship by encouraging their teammates throughout the activity and by showing respect to all participants, including congratulating the other team after the challenge.
❏ Students will reflect on the importance of teamwork and sportsmanship by identifying **3** things they learned about teamwork, **2** ways to show good sportsmanship, and **1** way to be a supportive teammate on the 3-2-1 reflection worksheet.

Materials Needed
❏ Lily pads (*use items like foam circles, poly spots, or pieces of cardboard to represent lily pads; you'll need about five lily pads per team – or adjust based on the distance across the 'river'*)
❏ Timer
❏ Boundary maker (*use cones or tape to outline the 'river' edges and designate starting and finishing points*)
❏ Markers
❏ 3-2-1 reflection sheets
❏ Pencils/pens

Session 7: Project Lead the Way
Leadership & Service

Student Learning Outcomes
❑ Students will define leadership and identify key characteristics/traits of effective leaders.
❑ Students will collaborate with peers to demonstrate leadership traits through role-play.
❑ Students will analyze and evaluate leadership behaviors through observation and discussion.
❑ Students will set actionable goals to enhance their leadership abilities.

Materials Needed
❑ Bulletin paper/whiteboard and markers
❑ Index cards (*for writing leadership characteristics/traits*)
❑ Timer/online stopwatch
❑ Student notebook journals/folders (*for 'Do Now' and 'Check for Understanding' assignments*)

Session 8: Brotherhood Member Presentation Finale: Preparation

Student Learning Outcomes
❏ Students will reflect on their personal growth and experiences in the group through creative and written expression.
❏ Students will articulate their goals and the steps needed to achieve them through a vision board activity.
❏ Students will express their reflections on the group experience through journaling.

Materials Needed

Vision Board:

❏ Post-test survey (*page 89*)
❏ Invitations for Brotherhood Membership Presentation (*sample email on page 82*)
❏ Brotherhood Oath index card
❏ Student notebook journals/folders

Vision Board:

❏ Poster board or large paper
❏ Markers, crayons, colored pencils
❏ magazines/stickers (*for pictures/words*)

Boys to Men:
Brotherhood Membership Presentation Finale

Student Learning Outcomes
❏ Students will reflect on their personal growth and experiences in the group through creative and written expression.
❏ Students will articulate their goals and the steps needed to achieve them through a vision board activity.
❏ Students will express their reflections on the group experience through journaling.

Materials Needed
❏ Any desired decorations
❏ Brotherhood Membership Certificates (page x)
❏ Desired music
❏ Participant Vision Boards
❏ Brotherhood Oath Index Cards
❏ Student Journals
❏ Programs/ QR code display for programs
❏ Any desired food/ snacks/ drinks for program

Appendix D
Group Exemplar Letters

Brotherhood Exemplar Email for Teachers

Greetings _____ [*Teacher's name or Grade level*]!

I'm excited to introduce Brotherhood, a new small group program we'll be launching for our upper elementary and middle school boys. Brotherhood is a culturally responsive and inclusive curriculum designed to support the unique needs of minority boys. The program provides a safe space where participants can develop essential social, emotional, and leadership skills while exploring their identities and building self-worth. Please read through the information below regarding the small group.

Brotherhood Small Group Objectives

By the end of the program, participants will be:

- ❏ equipped with tools to understand and manage emotions
- ❏ able to cultivate leadership qualities
- ❏ able to explore and celebrate their identities
- ❏ able to set meaningful goals, identify barriers, and create actionable steps to achieve success (both inside and outside the classroom)
- ❏ equipped to communicate effectively, collaborate with others, and address common challenges with peer pressure, bullying, and societal expectations.

Brotherhood Small Group Logistics

- ❏ **Duration**: The small group will meet for 8 sessions that will last approximately 30–45 minutes each.
- ❏ **Frequency**: The group will meet weekly during_____ [*insert time period*].
- ❏ **Finale**: The program will conclude with a special finale presentation celebrating the participants' growth and accomplishments. Parents and teachers are invited to attend (more information to come).

Teacher Request

As a teacher who works closely with our students, your insights are invaluable. If you know any boys who could benefit from this supportive and empowering environment, please complete this form _____ [*insert link to form or attach form*]. We hope to make this group a meaningful experience where each participant feels heard, valued, and prepared for their future.

Feel free to reach out with any questions or to discuss specific students.

Warm regards,

_____ [*your name*]

School Counselor

Brotherhood Exemplar Teacher Referral Form

This form can also be recreated using Google Forms, Qualtrics, or other technological platforms for ease of data collection.

Brotherhood Small Group Referral Form

Please complete this short referral form to refer students for the Brotherhood Small Group. If you have any questions, please feel free to email [*School Counselor's email/phone number*].

Teacher's name _____

Student name_____

Grade level _____

Reason for Referral *(please check all that apply)*

- ❏ Could benefit from additional mentorship.
- ❏ Demonstrates leadership potential but needs additional guidance/motivation.
- ❏ Struggles with confidence/social skills.
- ❏ Needs reinforcement in positive peer interactions.
- ❏ Shows academic potential but needs support/motivation.
- ❏ Other: _____.

Brief Explanation

Please describe why you feel this student would benefit from the Brotherhood Small Group.

Brotherhood Exemplar Parent/ Guardian Consent Form

Parent/Guardian Consent Form

Brotherhood Small Group Counseling Program

Dear Parent/Guardian,

We are excited to offer your child the opportunity to participate in the **Brotherhood Small Group**, a culturally responsive and inclusive small group program designed for boys. This group aims to support the unique needs of minority boys through engaging interactive sessions that focus on personal growth, leadership, and social-emotional skills.

About the Program

Brotherhood provides a safe space where boys can explore their identities, develop emotional regulation skills, build leadership abilities, and learn to navigate challenges such as peer pressure and bullying. Through experiential activities, discussions, and goal setting, the program equips participants with tools to succeed inside and outside the classroom. The group also emphasizes community engagement, fostering values of empathy, accountability, and responsibility.

Group Logistics

- ❏ **Duration**: The small group will meet for 8 sessions that will last approximately 30-45 minutes.
- ❏ **Frequency**: The group will meet weekly during _____ [*insert time period*].
- ❏ **Finale**: The program will conclude with a special finale presentation celebrating the participants' growth and accomplishments. Parents and teachers are invited to attend (more information to come).

Participation in the Brotherhood group is voluntary, and your consent is required for your child to join. Please complete and sign the form below to grant permission for your child's participation. If you have any questions or concerns, feel free to contact me at _____ [*School Counselor's email/phone number*].

Please complete the following and return to your child's teacher no later than _____ [*desired date*].

Student name: _____

Grade: ❏ 5th ❏ 6th ❏ 7th

Homeroom teacher: _____

    ❏ *Yes, I give permission* for my child to participate in the Brotherhood Small Group Counseling Program.

    ❏ *No, I do not give permission* for my child to participate.

Parent/Guardian name: _____

Parent/Guardian signature: _____

Date: _____

Contact Information (Optional):

Phone: _____

Email: _____

Thank you for allowing your child to participate in this empowering experience! We look forward to working with them and supporting their growth.

Sincerely,

_____ [*School Counselor's name*]

_____ [*School name*]

References and Further Resources

American School Counselor Association. (2019). *ASCA National Model: A Framework for School Counseling Programs* (4th ed.). Author.

American School Counselor Association. (2021). *ASCA Student Standards: Mindsets and Behaviors for Student Success*. Author.

Bryant, TB, Akom, AA, & Ginwright, S. (2021). Culturally responsive education and the Black male achievement gap. *Journal of Urban Education*, 56(2), 245–260.

Dimmitt, C, Carey, J, & Hatch, T. (2017). *Evidence-Based School Counseling: Making a Difference with Data-Driven Practices*. Corwin Press.

Eccles, JS, Midgley, C, Wigfield, A, & Buchanan, CM (2019). Development during adolescence: The impact of stage-environment fit on young adolescents' experiences in schools and families. *Journal of Research on Adolescence*, 29(3), 321–334.

Gay, G. (2021). *Culturally Responsive Teaching: Theory, Research, and Practice* (3rd ed.). Teachers College Press.

Hammond, Z. (2020). *Culturally Responsive Teaching and the Brain: Promoting Authentic Engagement and Rigor Among Culturally and Linguistically Diverse Students*. Corwin Press.

Jones, J, & Okun, T. (2019). Emotional development and the school experiences of minority boys. *Journal of Educational Psychology*, 111(3), 560–575.

Ladson-Billings, G. (2018). *The Dreamkeepers: Successful Teachers of African American Children* (3rd ed.). Jossey-Bass.

Reigeluth, CS, & Addis, ME (2020). Adolescent boys' resistance to hypermasculine norms: Implications for healthy development. *Psychology of Men & Masculinities*, 21(4), 567–576.

Sink, CA. (2016). *Comprehensive School Counseling Programs: K-12 Delivery Systems in Action*. Pearson.

Uhls, YT, Ellison, NB, & Subrahmanyam, K. (2017). The impact of social media on adolescent development. *Adolescent Medicine: State of the Art Reviews*, 28(1), 27–41.

Index

Pages in *italics* refer to figures, pages in **bold** refer to tables, and pages followed by "n" refer to notes.

For Product Safety Concerns and Information please contact our EU representative GPSR@taylorandffrancis.com
Taylor & Francis Verlag GmbH, Kaufingerstraße 24, 80331 München, Germany